Y0-BRN-303

MURDER AND MAYHEM IN THIS LAND, THE ONTONAGON

FORWARD

In looking at the history of any area one always likes to recall the progressive and innovative things of the past which point to the progress or contributions of an area to the total development of the country. There is a darker side to history, however, which though not pleasant, is a part of the story of an area.

It is not the place of the historian to speculate on the motives or reasons why an individual would seek to take another person's life, but it is a fact that from the first recorded taking of a life by a killer in Ontonagon County in 1854 there have been several homicides right down to the present, many of which left unanswered questions as to motive or even the guilt of the perpetrators. It is with this thought in mind that we will meet several killers/murderers in this volume about whom there is some question of their guilt. It is not the place of the historian to try to make opinion, but to report the circumstances of history as accurately as possible. It is up to you, the reader to draw your own conclusions about the cases you will read about.

We have tried to focus on those cases in which time provides a cushion from the occurrence in order to not "drag up old saws" so there will be no crimes discussed here that took place more recently than 1930. Perhaps this is a safe enough distance to look back from this new year of 1997 for we do seek to keep off the thin ice of human feelings.

As previously stated, we will confine this discussion to killings about which there is an unanswered question. There is no doubt in anybody's mind that the first murder in Ontonagon County in which Henry Hocking gunned down Patrick Dolan in the presence of numerous witnesses was a classic example of a cold-blooded frontier killing, though oddly enough, today Hocking would probably have stood trial on reduced charges of man slaughter rather than murder.

Another early incident in Ontonagon was the ax killing of Terril Johnson by James Ryan, a Rockland saloon keeper during the Minesota Mine riot of April, 1857. This was simply a situation where an ancient feud transplanted to the New world between the Catholic Irish and the Protestant Cornish boiled over with unfortunate outcomes. There is no question of who did what to whom in either of the above cases.

We will look to some of the lesser known cases, and as long as there are still unanswered questions about the accused killers or their guilt, (to paraphrase a statement made by one of the murderers we will meet in this volume), of the victims, we can say **their blood still runs.**

B.H. Johanson
Firesteel, Ontonagon, Michigan
1997

MURDER AND MAYHEM IN THIS LAND, THE ONTONAGON

CONTENTS

Copyright 1997
Bruce H. Johanson

Ontonagon, Michigan

CHAPTER ONE
THE JAILHOUSE HEROES

First, let the reader be clear about a few of the established facts in this case. It is common knowledge that the Village of Ontonagon, a thriving town whose sole industry and major employer was the Diamond Match Company that operated two mammoth sawmills and a box factory burned to the ground on August 25, 1896. It is also an established fact that during the course of this major tragedy, an event that reduced most of the private property in the town to ruin and placed every life in peril, many acts of heroism were certainly enacted. Accounts written after the great fire of 1896 tell of children leading fire-blinded adults to safety; of grief stricken mothers carrying the bodies of dead children about; of neighbor helping neighbor to save what they could before fleeing the wind-driven wall of flames that soon enveloped the town. Indeed, these acts of heroism were not limited to friend helping friend and neighbor aiding neighbor. At the County Jail, a scene was being enacted that would be indeed rare in the history of This Land, the Ontonagon.

There were, at the time of the fire, two men accused of murder awaiting trial in the County Jail. Indeed, the date of the trial was only a short time away. James Redpath, age 42, and Duncan Beveridge, age 38, both of whom had been accused of and charged with first-degree murder were incarcerated within the brick walls of the jail, and had been there for some time. On that fateful day in August a century ago when Ontonagon took fire, everyone in the village was so occupied with the task of saving their families and possessions, that the two prisoners were forgotten .... forgotten by everyone, that is, but the wife of Sheriff Silas Corbett. In those days, the Sheriff lived at the jail itself and often times the wife of the Sheriff would also prepare food for the prisoners. Sheriff Corbett was out of the village at this time, having left for another part of the county by train on his routine duties and HE HAD TAKEN THE JAIL KEYS WITH HIM!

Mrs. Corbett, seeing the houses taking fire in the next block hunted for a key to open the cells and release the prisoners who were in a panic. The walls of the jail were becoming hot to the touch, sparks were raining down on the wooden roof of the jailhouse, and Mrs. Corbett also had the additional problem of getting away to safety with her children and her aged mother who lived at the jail with the Corbett family.

At the height of all this excitement, a pretty younger woman appeared at the jail claiming to be the wife of Redpath, one of the prisoners. She demanded the immediate release of her husband before he burned, "Like an animal in a cage." Mrs. Corbett hastily explained the problem of the absent key and the two women, united in a common effort opened desk drawers, searched in corners and forgotten boxes until, lo and behold, a key that fit the cell door in which the two charged murderers was found. On release, Redpath and his female partner, as well as Beveridge made fast tracks to escape the fire. Mrs. Corbett was left to struggle with the rescue of her own family. The Sheriff's wife, now in near panic herself and confused by the thick smoke, led her mother and children off the street and soon found herself surrounded by burning brush in the cedar swamp (now the lower part of the "back" street near the current laundromat). Suddenly, out of the smoke two figures appeared .... Redpath and Beveridge! One took the children up in his arms and ordered Mrs. Corbett to follow. The other half carried, half dragged the old woman to the east up to the Pigeon Hill area where the fire did not reach. Having saved Mrs. Corbett and her family, the two men waited about in the area until the next morning when the Sheriff himself returned, then they voluntarily turned themselves in.

One has to wonder what sort of men were James Redpath and Duncan Beveridge? Who were they supposed to have murdered? Could someone who saved several lives in an act of heroism be capable of taking another life in a premeditated manner? This tale of murder in the Ontonagon country leads the reader on a long journey which will span over seven years.

To get the whole story, we have to back up a few year to 1889. At that time, the Diamond Match Company had its south-end headquarters in the town of Matchwood, then a part of Ontonagon Township (Matchwood Twp., would not be separated from Ontonagon Twp. until 1897). Cut over timberland was available as homestead property for a very small sum and on one John McDonald, "Jack" to those who knew him, had started a small homestead located along the D.S.S. & A. railroad tracks just east of the settlement of Matchwood. It seems that at some point in 1889, McDonald sold (there is some hint in the arrest warrants that he lost the homestead in a poker game) to James Redpath who in July of that summer moved into the 16 X 32" log house that McDonald had built on the property. Accompanying Redpath was a young woman of 21 named Maggie Flaherty, who lived with Redpath without benefit matrimonial status.

Redpath had a long acquaintanceship with a Duncan Beveridge, the two men having been partners in several business ventures for years. As soon as he had settled in, Redpath wrote to his friend Beveridge and suggested that he too come to

Matchwood and "take out" a homestead .... after all, the land was cheap and could only go up in value. Beveridge took his former partner up on the offer and shortly thereafter arrived, and with him was a young woman whom he introduced as Molly, his recent bride. The two couples set up housekeeping together in the small log house consisting of two rooms, a kitchen with an attached woodshed, and a "sitting room" one end of which they partitioned off into two 8x8 cubicles that served as the bedrooms. The Beveridges, being a bit more modest, hung a curtain at the end of their cubicle which was drawn at night. Redpath and his lady friend left their cubicle open.

The two couples got along fairly well, with the women taking care of the house and meals and also helping the men get in the hay. Jack McDonald, the former homesteader dropped in one day, saw the progress that had been made in his former home, and now regretted selling the place. Some accounts report that McDonald felt that he had been cheated out of it by Redpath. In any case, McDonald, a former lumberjack who seems to have been a strong man and a willing worker, offered to help Redpath and his partner get in the last of the hay, then to help Beveridge get up a cabin on the land next door on which he had filed a homestead claim. All McDonald wanted in return was a place to eat and sleep and some help in getting his shack up on his new homestead property across the railroad tracks from his former holding. All agreed to the plan and McDonald moved into the small house with the two couples. At night a cot was set up in the kitchen of the cabin for his use and the door between the kitchen and the sitting room was kept closed and latched at night. There seems to have been some apprehension on the part of the women about having the older bachelor lumberjack barge into their presence at night.

Now, there are two versions of just what took place on the night of November 11-12, 1889, but the one indisputable fact is that Molly Beveridge, the young wife of Duncan Beveridge, was shot in the head and killed; Maggie Flaherty was wounded gravely, and Duncan Beveridge was shot in the wrist and also received a bullet crease to his scalp. The **confessed** murderer was none other than Jack McDonald. The strange thing about this incident is that although McDonald had given something of a confession .... "I musta done it," he also claimed that he did not at all remember doing the deed. At his trial, which was held in Marquette County, his defense was somnambulism. McDonald testified that he had been asleep at the time he did the shooting! The murder weapon was a Winchester rifle which Redpath testified to have taken out of McDonald's hands at the scene of the crime. McDonald was found guilty and sentenced to serve time at Marquette State

Prison. In 1895, McDonald, after serving something short of five years, was released. New evidence had come forth by a new witness and McDonald was turned loose and warrants were issued for the arrest of James Redpath and Duncan Beveridge on the charge of murder!

This new evidence was the testimony of none other than Maggie Flaherty former mistress of James Redpath. Now Mrs. Brant Peterson of Eau Claire, Wisconsin, Maggie had come forth at this time to, in her own words, "set an innocent man free and to clear my conscience." She told a shockingly different version of the killing of Molly Beveridge .... a killing for which Jack McDonald had gone to prison in 1890. Her story ....

Maggie Flaherty Peterson, now at age 28, related much the same background: about taking up residence at the homestead in Matchwood. She related how McDonald had joined the couples and how the women had kept house and the men had done the heavy outside work. She and the late Molly Beveridge had pitched in with the hay making and later in the fall the work had indeed begun on the house for the Beveridges to move into.

Maggie's story differed, however, in the events of the morning of November 12 ... that at about 2:30 AM there had been a disturbance in the house. According to Maggie's story, the Beveridges were quarreling loudly. Molly Beveridge was heard to get out of bed. Only thin boards separated the two sleeping chambers and voices carried easily through the makeshift walls. "Where are you going?" Beveridge was heard to demand.

"I'm going away, and when I get away, I'm going to fix you plenty," shot back the voice of Molly Beveridge.

According to Maggie's story, there was a short pause; the sound of feet moving across the rough board of the floor of the cabin; then a **SHOT!**

Maggie related how she climbed out of bed, crawling over the awakening Redpath as her place was against the wall. She entered the sitting room and in the dim light of the kerosene lamp which was kept burning low at night, she saw Duncan Beveridge standing near the kitchen door with the Winchester rifle in his hands that was usually kept hanging on wooden pegs on the wall. On the floor near the wood stove which heated the cabin was the figure of Molly Beveridge, hands over her face, in a prostrate position, obviously mortally wounded. Maggie could see by the dim light a hole in the side of Molly's face from which a gray substance was oozing out onto the floor.

Upon seeing Maggie standing in the comer of the room, Beveridge turned the gun on her, levered another cartridge into the chamber, and fired from the hip hitting Maggie in the left thigh. The bullet shattered her upper leg bone and she fell to the floor. By this time, according to Maggie's testimony, Jim Redpath had jumped from the bed and seizing the gun from his friend's hands he cried out, "My God, Duncan, what have you done? How are you going to get out of this one?"

Beveridge, according to Maggie, made a curious reply ... "It is better that I did this than let her send me up ... What's the matter with pinning it on that man,?" as he nodded towards the kitchen where the sleeping Jack McDonald lay on his cot.

Evidently, all the commotion had awakened the older man who now began to pound on the LATCHED kitchen door asking what was going on ..... what was all the shooting about? Beveridge called through the door that they were simply shooting at some lynx through the window and to go back to sleep.

Maggie then related how the two men stripped the street clothes off of the dying woman, using a jackknife to cut off the two corsets she wore. She was then dressed in her nightgown and left lying on the floor where she had first fallen. Her street clothes were put in the stove and burned.

Maggie now told that the two men picked her up, not too gently, and threw her back in bed. Her broken leg was causing her great pain and she was on the verge of fainting, but the two men charged her to keep her mouth shut about the events of the night or they would "get her too." She was instructed to stick by the story that would shortly unfold, or else!

Having thus arranged the evidence to suit their purpose, Redpath and Beveridge called out to the sleeping Jack McDonald and opened the kitchen door so he could enter the small room where the mortally wounded Molly Beveridge lay dying on the floor.

McDonald entered the room, squinted at the figure on the floor, then inquired what had happened. McDonald would have to have been rather slow witted and easily led, if the rest of the story told my Maggie Flaherty Peterson is to be believed.

"It looks like you killed Molly," stated Beveridge, handing the gun to Jack. "The best thing for you to do is to skip."

"I don't remember doing it. I musta been asleep," replied the still drowsy lumberjack. McDonald dropped into a chair and put his head in his hands, rifle on his lap, making no attempt to escape. Redpath took the rifle away from McDonald and then volunteered to go into Matchwood to try to find the company doctor and bring him back to look to the shooting victims.

Maggie's story continues: after she heard Redpath leave the house, she lay in great pain for a time, then she heard two more spaced shots. She told of being quite hazy, due to the intensity of the pain in her leg and she may have even passed out. The next thing she remembered was being jostled a bit and awakening to find that four men were carrying her, mattress and all so as not to move her broken leg, from the house to the railroad tracks where an eastbound train had been flagged down. Redpath was there too, as well as Beveridge who had a bloody bandage on his wrist and another bandage around his head. No further information was given to her except that Molly Beveridge was still breathing but that her wound was mortal. In fact Molly Beveridge did die later that morning and Jack McDonald was arrested and charged with her murder.

McDonald stood trial and on the testimony given by Redpath and Beveridge was found guilty. They related how McDonald had burst through the kitchen door, grabbed the rifle off the wall, firing wildly into the Beveridge bed chamber wounding Beveridge and also delivering the mortal wound to Molly Beveridge. According to the testimony given by Redpath and Beveridge, McDonald then turned the rifle on Redpath, but missed and hit Maggie in the leg before being disarmed by Redpath. McDonald had entered a plea of innocent due to sleepwalking, but was found guilty and sent to prison.

Maggie Flaherty had spent a year and a week in the hospital at Marquette, recovering from her leg wound. When she left the hospital, her left leg was shorter than her right and she had to walk with a cane. The reader is reminded that pinning a shattered fracture was not possible in that day given the state of medicine in the 19th century .... in fact, it is something short of miraculous that her leg was not amputated!

After her discharge from the hospital, Maggie rejoined her lover, Redpath, where he had again joined into a partnership with his old friend Duncan Beveridge in a "business venture" operating a "house of ill fame" at Marinette, Wisconsin. Maggie was immediately employed as a "hostess" in this establishment and once again, began practicing the "oldest profession" with which she was seemingly quite experienced.

Evidently, there was trouble almost from the first between Maggie and the other girls. Maggie, according to testimony given at the trial of James Redpath, drank too much, made trouble, and bragged openly to the other girls about her past with Redpath. Duncan Beveridge finally asked her to pack up her things and leave. Maggie informed Beveridge that she only took orders from her former lover, Redpath. Infuriated, Beveridge asked his partner to deal with his girl. Redpath took charge of Maggie and "whipped her so bad" that she was unable to get out of bed for nearly two weeks. As soon as she was able, Maggie fled the house.

In the summer of 1895, Maggie Flaherty Peterson, now married to a lumber man from Eau Claire, Wisconsin, came forward and related her version of the events of that fateful night nearly six years before.

Redpath was found and arrested. Though, according to Maggie's story, he had been only an accomplice in the murder of Molly Beveridge, he was charged with murder along with his former partner Duncan Beveridge who was extradited from Lake County, Minnesota where, in 1896, he was operating another saloon and sporting house.

After surviving the burning of Ontonagon and saving the Sheriff's wife and family from a death by flames, the jailhouse heroes were taken into custody a second time and transferred to the jail at Bessemer in Gogebic County as Ontonagon not only had no jail in which to keep them, but no courthouse in which to try them.

On November 19, 1896, James Redpath went on trial for his part in the murder of Molly Beveridge. On December 9, 1896, a motion to Quash was made by the defense attorney and granted by Judge Norman Haire. Redpath was free!

Duncan Beveridge himself came to trial on February 23, 1897. James Redpath was called as a defense witness for his friend and Redpath testified that he had NEVER been married: the woman who had appeared at the burning jail representing herself as his wife was only one of several women, Maggie Flaherty included, who had shared his bed through the years.

When put on the stand, Duncan Beveridge also testified that the woman who had called herself Molly Beveridge, the victim, had not been his legal wife either ... she was simply a girl he had met in Chicago. He had asked her to live with him but she had insisted on something more substantial, such as marriage. It seems that Molly's stepmother had drawn up a contract, of sorts, in which Molly would provide the services of a wife in turn for the privilege of being able to represent herself as Mrs. Beveridge (whatever that is supposed to mean)! Beveridge stated that to the best of his knowledge, Molly had been buried at Bessemer after her death the morning after the shooting. He hadn't bothered to visit the grave, if it was indeed there.

Customers from the establishment the two partners had operated at Marinette were called to testify. Several testified that Maggie Flaherty was loud and abusive when drinking and she was said to have often cursed a man named McDonald for shooting her and crippling her as she was.

Judge Haire instructed the jury with these words ..... "The defense has introduced evidence to show that the witness, Maggie Flaherty Peterson, has been a woman of unchaste character .... it is a general rule of law that a lack of chastity in a woman cannot be used for the purpose of impeaching credibility; and you are warned, therefore, against considering such testimony as affecting the credibility of this witness." In short, Maggie's past was not to be considered in whether her testimony was reliable or not.

It is a certainty, given the past history of both James Redpath and Duncan Beveridge, that these two were guilty of many things, but was murder one of them? Was Maggie telling the truth about the death of Molly Beveridge, or was she a vindictive troublemaker trying to get even with her former lover and his partner? Perhaps we will never know for sure, but the jury trial was concluded on March 4, 1897 and Beveridge was discharged. It is left to you, the reader to decide what really happened.

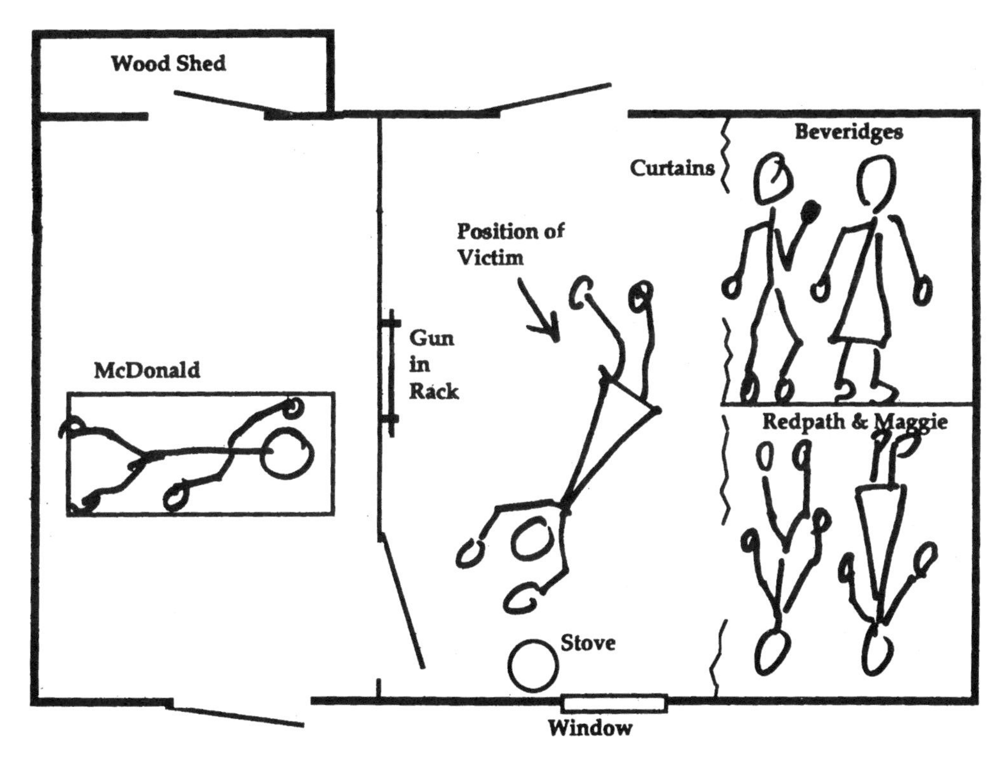

Diagram of the crime scene at the Matchwood homestead where Molly Beveridge was killed in 1889.

CHAPTER TWO
THE MURDER THAT WASN'T A MURDER

Walking into the 8th grade Civics class, I opened my briefcase, took out a small .32 calibre Smith & Wesson revolver, and laid it on the desk in front of the class. Immediately interest in the day's lesson picked up. I called Tommy up to the front of the room. Tommy had been assigned the job of being the County Prosecutor in a mock trial we were going to role-play in class that day.

"What a neat old gun .... can I touch it?" asked Tommy. I told him not only could he touch it, but that this little pistol was a very important piece of evidence in the case he was going to prosecute in class that day. As the boy examined the gun, I explained to him that this gun had actually been used in a killing... that the last time this gun had been fired was in 1893 and that it's last shot killed an Ontonagon County Deputy Sheriff

Yes, this is a rather extreme way to make history come alive to young people, but the incident is true. By the way, Tommy got his conviction in the mock trial that day. The trial we acted out in class was based on the case which you are about to read ....

Tuesday evening, November 21, 1893, the town of Trout Creek, at the extreme eastern edge of Ontonagon County, was the scene of a "murder most foul," as described in the words of the *Ontonagon Herald* four days after the incident.

Trout Creek was a mill town nestled alongside the D.S.S.& A. Railroad tracks that traversed the width of the County. As in most of the outlying towns of Ontonagon County, the law was represented by a resident deputy sheriff and also by a local constable, as was the case with Trout Creek. The local deputy at Trout Creek was George Davidson, a soft-spoken lawman who was by no means gun-happy. Davidson, who stood 6' 5" seldom had to draw his weapon to make arrests because of his intimidating physical stature. He was happily married, had two grown daughters, and had been a resident of Trout Creek almost since the town was established.

Deputy Davidson was just sitting down to supper in his home when word was brought to him that Alex Enos, a local character who earned his living ostensibly by trapping, was trying to kill one of his girls. Actually, Enos owned and operated a house of ill fame at the edge of town. A man of 24 years of age, Enos had three "soiled doves" working for him at his establishment and evidently one of the girls had taken it into her head to leave her employment in the company of one of her gentleman clients. Enos, who also had a rude bar set up in his establishment, had been drinking all day, and upon learning of the departure of his girl, went after her in a drunken rage. Catching up with her at the railroad station, he drove her back towards his house at gun point firing shots at random to lend emphasis to his curses which could be heard far and wide.

Davidson grabbed his handcuffs and headed for Enos' place. On the way, he encountered the train crew of the D.S.S. & A. train that was in the station loading passengers and freight and asked them to accompany him as a sort of posse. It was not at all unusual in those days for lawmen to recruit and deputize help whenever and wherever it was needed. The trainmen went along without question. In those rough and tumble days in Trout Creek, every man was expected to do his part to keep the streets safe for the public. The railroad engineer, Pat O'Brien who had been hastily recruited as a special deputy evidently knew Deputy George Davidson and was on a first name basis with him. Also in the group of railroaders was Fireman McCarthy and an unnamed Conductor.

Upon reaching the Enos place, the four men entered. Enos, quite intoxicated, was threatening his three girls with a Winchester rifle and was firing into the ceiling as the girls ran about upstairs, bullets tearing splinters out of the floor as they fled the hail of lead coming from down below. Big George Davidson calmly walked over to Enos, placed his ham-like hand on his shoulder, and asked for the gun. Enos turned, saw the posse, and knew that he was in trouble. He refused to surrender his gun, at which point Davidson suggested that they retire to a room behind the bar to talk things over. Davidson instructed the others to wait in the barroom while he tried to calm Enos down. The two men entered the room and sat on the bed. George Davidson, in a soft, reassuring way, talked to Enos in his deep rumbling voice and seemed to calm him a bit. Slowly, the Deputy removed the rifle from Enos' hands and took out his handcuffs, all the time speaking in a low tone.

Suddenly, Enos became aware of the handcuffs. Out of nowhere, a small Smith &Wesson .32 calibre pistol appeared in his fight hand! Davidson saw the pistol and grabbed for Enos' hand. Pat O'Brien, the railroad engineer came running.

"Pat, take that revolver!" were George Davidson's last words. As O'Brien reached for the gun in Enos' right hand, Enos twisted his wrist and fired. O'Brien jumped back momentarily, a bullet having torn through his left hand. Again Enos twisted his wrist, this time to the left. The pistol was fired again and the big

Deputy slumped to the floor, a bullet in his abdomen. Enos, now free of the Deputy, turned the gun on O'Brien again and fired. The engineer sustained a flesh wound in his side. Totally out of control now, Enos lowered the muzzle of the pistol towards the floor and fired point blank into the head of the stricken Deputy putting a bullet into the edge of Davidson's mouth and out the other side of his skull. Enos fired a last wild shot emptying his gun (a five shot revolver...not a six-shooter). Everything had happened in mere seconds.

Quickly, Enos was overpowered by Fireman McCarthy who came flying into the room upon hearing the first shot. The handcuffs were pried from Davidson's dead hand and placed on Enos, who was then not any too gently taken downtown and turned over to the Trout Creek constable by the deputized trainmen.

Enos seems not to have been any too popular in Trout Creek, or perhaps it was the high regard in which the townspeople held Deputy Davidson. Within an hour, there was talk of a lynching. Enos was hurriedly taken to Ewen and held there until Sheriff Francis came down from Ontonagon (by way of Sidnaw on the train) to pick him up the next day. The jail in Ewen had to be kept under armed guard all night because of threats being made to storm the place and string Enos up to the nearest lamp post!

Now there is really no mystery about who killed Deputy Sheriff George Davidson ..... the person responsible was Alexander Enos, but was it murder? Enos did one thing right. After spending a night in jail, he retained the law firm of F. C. Chamberlain and C.O. Trumbull of Ewen for his defense counsel. Trumbull, who has been described by some as the Clarence Darrow of the North pulled every legal trick in the book to secure his client's release. He charged police brutality. Enos had indeed been badly beaten by the posse on the evening of the killing, but perhaps one shouldn't blame them too much for, after all, one of their party had been shot twice and Enos had indeed killed Deputy Davidson right in front of them. The local newspaper dismissed the bruises Enos sustained with the words:

"Enos has a rather boyish appearance, with dark hair and eyes, and but for a badly disfigured nose and discolored face, would be rather good-looking. He wears a small black moustache and stands about five feet eight." (*Ontonagon Herald*, November 25, 1893)

The *Ewen Weekly Recorder* of November 25, 1893, described Enos thusly: "Enos is a short, thick-set, brutal, unintelligent fellow. He is a Canadian Frenchman. He had kept a dive at Trout Creek for some time and has caused several disturbances. He did not appear to realize the nature of the charge against him, and was as unconcerned as if he had shot only a dog. He is either a cold-blooded, heartless murderer, or he is an imbecile."

The *Weekly Recorder* further stated," .... Many think it a pity that capital punishment is not allowed in Michigan. They think hanging is the fate which Enos should get. Many good law-abiding citizens declared that they would like to help lynch him."

Attorney Trumbull claimed excessive bias on the part of the local press. He filed affidavits with the Circuit Court showing that the press had already convicted Enos, calling him a murderer before he had even stood trial. Within a week of the shooting, the townspeople of Trout Creek burned Enos' house to the ground, thus destroying any forensic evidence that may have yet remained within its walls germane to the forthcoming trial.

By the time the trial came about, Trumbull had filed petitions for a change in venue, claiming that Enos couldn't possibly get a fair trial in Ontonagon County. Trial was scheduled for February 13, 1894 in the Ontonagon County' Courthouse, Judge Norman Haire, Presiding. The Ontonagon County Prosecutor was none other than the venerable W. Worth Wendell who some have called the "William Jennings Bryan of Ontonagon County."

Right from the beginning, Defense Attorney Trumbull's strategy seems to have been to challenge as many prospective jurors as possible. If he could exhaust the supply of jurors, perhaps he could win the change of venue that he considered essential to the defense of his client, Enos. The regular panel of 24 prospective jurors was soon exhausted, so the Sheriff was ordered by Judge Haire to obtain ONE HUNDRED additional tradesmen! Trumbull soon challenged these, and a second hundred were sent for, then yet a third! Never before had jury selection become such a drawn out process for a local trial. As jury members were finally selected, they were sequestered in the Centennial Hotel (located near the Auto Parts store at the lower end of River Street) but it was several days before a jury was agreed to. The Sheriff was actually forced to find jurors by waiting at the railroad station for the train to come in, then to button hole strangers getting off the train ... traveling salesmen and such. It was simply impossible to find anyone in Ontonagon County who had not formed an opinion about the case, given the coverage in the local newspapers so a jury of virtual strangers to the County was finally seated.

Enos entered a plea of not guilty of murder and claimed that the gun had gone off by accident. He further stated that the successive shots had been fired without the intention of hitting anyone (but he had killed Davidson and wounded another man twice). Attorney Trumbull made the claim that Deputy Davidson and Enos had been intimate friends and that Enos had no possible reason to want Davidson dead; therefore Davidson's death had been accidental because **there was no motive for the killing**. By legal definition, murder requires premeditation, and therefore a motive. Since no motive could be shown, Enos couldn't be guilty of murder.

Over thirty witnesses were called, including Enos' father, Joseph Enos from Cheboygan, Michigan. Lil Langtry of Trout Creek was Trumbull's star witness for the defense. Miss Langtry testified as to Enos' sterling character and his admiration for the man whom he had killed. Apparently the strategy of disclaiming any possible motive for murder worked, because Judge Haire reduced the charges.

In the end, Enos was found guilty, not of murder, but of manslaughter. He was sent to Marquette State Prison in 1894 and evidently was a model prisoner. He was released in 1901 after serving a little over seven years.

Of special interest is an oil painting, done by Enos while he was in prison. In 1898, Alexander Enos sent his painting to the Ontonagon County clerk. His painting depicted the Ontonagon County Courthouse which Enos had painted from memory. The painting clearly shows the courthouse as it appeared in 1894, two years before it was gutted by the Great Fire that destroyed the village of Ontonagon. Enos, who had three years yet to serve had vivid memories of the building in which he has stood trial for one of the most publicized homicides in Ontonagon County History.

"By the Killer's Hand," this painting by Alex Enos, slayer of Ontonagon County Deputy Sheriff George Davidson, painted while he was serving time at Marquette State Prison. Enos was reportedly a model prisoner and was released in 1901.

Picture Courtesy of Ontonagon County Historical Society

CHAPTER THREE
MASS CITY MAYHEM

It was payday evening at the Mass Consolidated Mining Company. At that time, Mass Consolidated was the major employer in the small mining camp of Mass City, Michigan, just over the ridge from the older community of Greenland.

Mass City, a boom town, was in its fifth year of existence. Typical of the day, the business district consisted of a variety of saloons, several hotels, and a pool room. Mass City even had a gun-toting Marshall who, at the first sign of trouble, drew first and asked questions afterwards.

Home to people from all corners of the globe, Mass City served as the residence place for many employees of the Mass Consolidated Mining Company. There was a Chinese laundry, an Italian Boardinghouse, the traditional Cornishmen bosses and Irish laborers, and more recently, the Finns who were relatively new to the United States fleeing Russian oppression in their homeland in Northern Europe.

N.I. Bobrikov, the Governor General of the Duchy of Finland, a part of the Russian empire, was the appointee of Czar Nicholas to oversee this province of his domain and to "pacify" the population. Because of his oppressive tactics, Bobrikov was so hated by the Finns that the Finnish-American League had commissioned a special cuspidor made of brass with a picture of Bobrikov in the bottom. These spittoons were frequently found in the saloons in mining settlements and logging towns where Finnish immigrants settled in the United States.

It seems that on the 16th of June, 1904, a young Finnish patriot named Eugen Schauman took it upon himself to assassinate the Russian tyrant. When news of this event reached Mass City two days later, half a world away, there was cause for much jubilation among the Finnish-Americans. The death of the Governor-General of Finland, coupled with payday at Mass Consolidated made for a great deal of merry making in Mass City that evening. All of the saloons and refreshment parlors were doing a booming business on the evening of June 18, and Korbi's Saloon was only one of the many doing a landfall business, thanks to the late Governor General.

John Korbi, the saloon owner, had a past history that included being an inmate in the Marquette Prison as a result of a conviction for a shooting incident in Republic, Michigan. Korbi had served four years and had then moved to the new town of Mass City. Unlike some of the Mass City saloon keepers such as Henry

Barbera, a Bavarian who had a well kept establishment on the ridge, Korbi was notorious for continuing to serve customers who were well into their cups, taking their last dime.

Korbi had a stepson, Gust Pertunnen, who was working in the saloon that evening serving drinks at the bar and serving as the "bouncer" when the need came up. About 7:00 p.m. John Kangass, already well on his way to sailing against the wind, arrived at the Korbi Saloon. Kangass had evidently been making the rounds and Korbi's was to be just one of his many watering spots that evening. In a short time, Kangass became quite quarrelsome and belligerent. He broke several glasses by dropping them on the floor and then loudly refused to pay for them when reproached by the management. At some point, another bar patron, tiring of Kangass' loud threats against the world and his foul language knocked him down. Kangass staggered to his feet and drew a jackknife from his pocket. John Korbi stepped in and took it away from him and Gust Pertunnen did his thing and put Kangass out the back door of the saloon in a most forceful manner, not sparing the babbling Kangass' feelings while doing it.

Kangass stumbled around outside the building and reentered the saloon by the front door and was just as quickly escorted right back out again by Pertunnen by the scruff of his neck. Kangass was gone only a short time when he again tried to come back in the saloon. This time, his attempt to join the celebrator's and drinkers was anticipated by bouncer Gust Pertunnen who met Kangass at the front door to bar his entry. The two men had words and scuffled a bit, when Kangass, suddenly and without warning grabbed the bouncer by the shoulder with his left hand, and slashed Pertunnen with a long knife which had materialized in his right hand from out of nowhere. The knife cut into Gust's left side, passing through a rib and around the front of his body. The knife was stopped by coming up against a suspender buckle, but had opened a gash fully 11 inches long across Pertunnen's abdomen.

The injured Pertunnen, with a look of shock on his face clutched his belly as blood streamed between his fingers and down his shirt front onto the floor. He exclaimed, in English, "Jesus, I am stabbed!"

In the confusion following the incident, all attention was focused on the injured man and Kangass was pushed outside. Evidently Kangass, even in his drunken state missed his hat and tried to reenter the saloon to retrieve it. He was again put out, so he ambled up the street and was met by Marshall Tom Cooney who was on routine street patrol. Cooney noticed that Kangass was hatless (no man ever went hatless in those days) and seemed quite nervous, but he was also quite drunk.

Cooney stopped Kangass and searched him, finding a bloody knife in one of his coat pockets. Kangass was dragged back to the saloon from which a great commotion was erupting and Marshall Cooney charged two bystanders to "watch him," while he entered the confusion within. Cooney was no sooner out of sight when Kangass slipped away unnoticed by the would-be guards who were distracted by the shouts and noise within the Korbi Saloon where Pertunnen lay dying. The lawman found Kangass only a short distance away, lying on the ground in a vacant lot quite out of sorts. He was taken to the Greenland jail and soon to Ontonagon for his own safety, as there was already talk of a lynching.

The question arises as to just who did the deed? Pertunnen died as a result of blood loss about 30 hours later leaving a wife and one child; Pertunnen was only 28 years of age. The suspect, Kangass, was age 26 and had a wife and two children in Finland .... he had been in the United States for about three years.

Korbi, the saloon owner, testified at the trial that Kangass had indeed wielded the knife and done the deed, though his testimony had a shadow cast upon it by the fact that he himself was an ex-convict who had served time for a violent act. Mrs. Korbi, wife of the saloon keeper testified that she had been in the room at the time of the attack and had seen Kangass raise his arm to strike, though she hadn't actually seen a knife. The circumstantial evidence of the town Marshall having found a bloody knife on Kangass seemed quite incriminating. This was before the days of blood typing in forensic crime detecting; further, the knife itself was not Kangass', but belonged to another Finnish miner in the community who, by the time of the trial had hastily returned to Finland!

John Kangass, the accused, testified in his own behalf. His English was quite limited and he didn't seem to comprehend the gravity of the charges against him or of the trial proceedings. He stated that he had no recollection of the crime whatsoever ... he remembered purchasing five bottles of beer for one dollar at the Korbi Saloon but that his mind was a blank any further than that ... he did recall that the saloon was a "rough house" that evening.

Pertunnen, the victim, made no incrimination against Kangass, though he lived for several hours after the incident, saying only, "He did stab me." Who was meant by the pronoun 'he' was never made clear by the victim himself.

Defense Attorney Oscar J. Larson claimed that in the crowded saloon, anyone could have done the deed and blamed it on the drunk and defenseless Kangass who had been knocked down and thrown out twice.

The defense also made a plea to the court that Kangass, who had been served in an intoxicated state by the disreputable Korbi could not be found guilty of murder,

CHAPTER FOUR
THE MINSTREL MURDER

This story begins on Sunday morning, March 26, 1911. Mr. Charles Stannard of Greenland, having been out late the previous night and morning had arrived at the home he shared with his wife, Laura, and their four children about 4:00 AM, and he was quite out of sorts.

Upon arising that morning, Laura Stannard and her 14-year-old daughter, Elaine, decided to teach Father a lesson. They blackened his face with shoe black, much as a minstrel show performer, then went downstairs and boasted to the domestic maid, Miss Dolly Hammes about doing it. When Mr. Stannard arose later that morning and saw his face in a mirror, he immediately surmised that his wife had something to do with it. Stannard went downstairs about 10:00, but he was in a foul mood. He entered the kitchen, threw a chair at his 16-year-old son, Alvah, and then engaged in a bitter quarrel with his wife. He then took his place at the breakfast table and was hurriedly served his morning coffee by the maid.

Now it seems that Laura Stannard had grown quite tired of her husband's frequent social drinking and had secretly sent away, through the Montgomery Ward Catalog for a patent medicine which was supposed to "cure the drinking habit,"in the words of the advertisement. Of course, all manner of promised cures for all manner of ills from liver problems to baldness were promised by various patent medicine vendors in that day before the ingredients had to be listed on medicine labels. That very morning she had decided that the time had come to "cure the drinking habit" of her husband and she had poured some yellow powder in her husband's empty coffee cup and told the maid that when her husband appeared, to pour his coffee over the powder and serve it to him. The cup was then placed on the warming oven of the kitchen range. When Charles came into the room, the maid did as she had been ordered. Charles took one mighty swig of the coffee, then another, and then began to spit the liquid out on the floor. He complained out loud of a strange bitter taste to his coffee and said to the maid, "What are you trying to do ... Poison me?" Complaining about his coffee, however, was not unusual as Charles definitely preferred his wife's coffee to that brewed by the maid.

Dolly the maid took the cup from Charles and poured it into the sink and Charles saw undissolved lumps of the yellow powder in the cup. He was quickly offered a fresh cup of coffee right from the pot on the stove and complained no more until a few minutes later when he arose from the table, spoke of feeling ill, and went upstairs to lie down. He was taken by a violent convulsion shortly after. Dr. Fred Larned, the Adventure Consolidated Mining Company doctor was summoned and when he attended Charles, the man was resting quietly. Dr. Larned, having no hint of what to look for left instructions that if the convulsions reoccurred, he was to be summoned at once and then left the Stannard residence. Charles had several more attacks, but the doctor was not summoned again, and, in the presence of his friend and neighbor, Sam Goard, Charles Stannard passed away in terrible agony at about 2:30 PM.

Because of the suddenness of Stannard's passing, the coroner was summoned and after hearing Goard's account of Stannard's last hours, refused to sign the death certificate until an autopsy had been performed. Within a week a coroners jury was convened at the railroad depot at Greenland and the following statement was issued .... **Charles Stannard of the Township of Greenland came to his death on the 26th day of March, 1911 from strychnia poisoning administered by the hand of Mrs. Laura Stannard.**

Thus began one of the most sensational murder cases ever tried in Northern Michigan. There was a long incarceration in the old county Jail for the accused, Laura Stannard, who was denied bail. Because of the prominence of the family, a long trial which involved expert witnesses was forthcoming and among the regular witnesses were the Stannard's children...one of the first times that children had been placed on the witness stand in Ontonagon County. The final result was a verdict which left many questions unanswered, even to this day.

After several months in jail, Laura Stannard went to trial in October of 1911. The Ontonagon County Prosecutor was John Jones, but to assure the most effective prosecution, W.A. Burritt of Hancock was retained by the County as a Special Prosecutor to actually handle the trial proceedings, assisted by Judge Van Slyck of Ontonagon. The Circuit Court Judge was A.C. Flannigan. Mrs. Stannard's attorney of record was Chester Brown who was assisted by the well known legal defense team of O'Brien and LeGendre of Laurium. (Patrick H. O'Brien was the nemesis of Calumet & Hecla winning huge judgments against that company in several compensation cases...his reputation throughout the Copper Country is still legendary).

Laura Stannard was a colorful defendant. She came well dressed to the trial and during the first day she wore black gloves and kept a handkerchief to her face, weeping constantly and frequently uttering pathetic sounds of remorse. Her own attorneys had to interrupt their questioning of witnesses to ask their client to try to control herself as her weeping and wailing made it difficult to hear the witnesses responses.

Mrs. Stannard was permitted visitors upon the conclusion of her first day in court, and those who knew her remarked about how wasted and thin she appeared. She claimed to have have lost nearly 25 pounds during the almost five months of her confinement. The reporter for the local press, Claude D. Riley, noted that Mrs. Stannard wore three diamond rings on her "wasted and delicate hands." It was also noted that Laura carried a cushion into court with her to sit on. The hardwood chairs of the courtroom may have left something to be desired in the way of comfort. Embroidered on the pillow was the motto, "Two Hearts Beat As One," and below this appeared two embroidered hearts joined by an arrow passing through them. One of her diamond rings consisted of a plain setting of two small diamonds taken out of a set of diamond earrings her late husband had given her for Christmas only two years before. She had ordered the ring made after her husband's death.

Testimony from the domestic maid, Grace "Dolly" Hammes, was very incriminating for Mrs. Stannard. The maid testified that Charles Stannard had been out late the night before his death, returning about 4:00 in the morning to the couple's home. When Laura arose that morning, she summoned her daughter, Elaine, age 14, and together they blackened Charlie's face with boot black while he lay asleep in his drunken stupor. The maid then testified that Mrs. Stannard had put a yellow powder in Charlie's favorite coffee cup and directed the maid to pour his coffee on the powder and serve it to him when he came to breakfast. Laura Stannard had assured the maid that the powder was "as harmless as cornstarch."

The maid also stated that when Stannard did put in his appearance that morning, he went straight to the cellar and brought up two quarts of beer, which he drank, then threw the chaff at his son and got into a quarrel with his wife about the face blackening incident. After consuming the beer, he started on his morning coffee, but complained almost at once about the bitter taste. She reinforced the facts known about the case already .... that after drinking a swallow or two of a fresh cup of coffee, he complained of not feeling well and went back upstairs. Shortly thereafter, the maid heard Mr. Stannard cry out in pain and went to tell Mrs. Stannard who was in another part of the house. Laura reportedly told the maid to "Let the damn fool cry!" The maid checked on Stannard and found him doubled up with pain and in violent convulsion. He suffered two more attacks within a three minute period in her presence. All this time, Laura Stannard remained downstairs and did not come up to the bedroom to check on her husband.

Dolly Hammes then made a statement which was very damaging to Laura

Stannard. She testified that Laura Stannard had told her to "forget about the powder," and stick to the story that she would lay out. At this point in the maid's testimony, Laura Stannard rose from her seat and sobbed, "Oh Dolly .... Dolly!"

Mr. Sam Goard, the neighbor who had been with Charles when he died, testified next. He stated that he stopped over when he heard that Charles was ill (how quickly news must have traveled in the small town of Greenland in those days). He told about how he had sat by Charlie's bedside. In the presence of this friend and neighbor, Laura Stannard brought a pitcher of water and offered a glass to her husband. Charlie refused to drink from his wife's hand, claiming that she was trying to poison him. When Sam held the glass, Charlie drank the water.

Judge Flannigan at this point ruled that all exclamations made by the deceased from the time he drank his morning coffee until his death were not allowable as evidence, as Mr. Stannard's competence was in doubt during this time. **This ruling was considered a great victory for the defense.**

Expert witnesses called by the prosecution included Dr. Victor C. Vaughn of Ann Arbor, Dean of the University of Michigan Medical School. Vaughn was a recognized expert in the effects of strychnine poison on humans and animals. It was Dr. Vaughn's considered opinion that Charles Stannard had died from strychnine poison and had suffered all the symptoms of such poisoning. His testimony was reinforced by the testimony of a second expert witness, Dr. Warden B. Hill from the Medical Department of Marquette University at Milwaukee. There was no challenge from the defense, so it was generally conceded that the cause of Stannard's death was unnatural and due to poison. The crime laboratory's report was reviewed and indicated that Stannard's liver and kidneys had been virtually laced with the substance.

Elaine, the fourteen-year-old daughter was called as a witness for the Prosecution to reinforce the maid's story of the face blackening incident and powder in the coffee. Elaine had been present at the table while her father drank his coffee. The clever cross-examination by Laura Stannard's attorney, LeGendre, however, began to turn the feelings in the community from one of loathing to one of pity for the accused. Claude Riley, reporting for the *Ontonagon Herald* of October 28, 1911 gave the following account:

LeGendre: Do you remember moving into the house where your father died?

Elaine: Yes, sir. Three or four years ago.

LeGendre: Was your mother keeping boarders constantly?

Elaine: Yes, sir.

LeGendre: When?
Elaine: When he (my father) was drunk.

Other damaging testimony given by the daughter of the deceased to the case of the Prosecution raised great feeling in the community for the plight of the poor abused wife of the late Charles Stannard.

LeGendre: Did your father ever strike your mother?
Elaine: Yes, Sir.
LeGendre: Do you remember any particular time?
Elaine: Sometimes he would whip Mama...strike her in the face or somewhere ... pull her earrings 'till her ears bled.
LeGendre: Did he (your father) have a gun in the house?
Elaine: Yes, Sir.
LeGendre: Do you remember anything particular about this gun?
Elaine: One day, he was cleaning the gun and said that there wouldn't be any Mama when I came home from school ... (At this point, the child burst into tears on the witness stand.)

Further cross-examination of Elaine brought out her testimony of some mysterious tablets which her father had taken after drinking. Elaine said that he would place a tablet on his tongue, then swallow some water. She also told of how her father would search the house for her mother's money which was hidden away in several safe places throughout the household. She told of one incident when her father had found a bottle of whiskey belonging to her Grandfather Chynoweth and had consumed all but "a teeny bit in the bottom of the bottle."

Alvah, the 17-year old son of the deceased was called next. He corroborated his sister's testimony during cross-examination about his father's abusive manner of behavior when drinking. He did add, under cross examination, which was damaging for the defense, that he had been the one to go to summon Dr. Fred Larned at his suffering father's request. His mother had refused to send for the doctor, but when she learned that he (Alvah) had left the house, his mother had run out into the yard, possibly to stop him, but seeing he was too far up the street, she had cried out so the neighbors would surely hear, "Hurry, Alvah, get the doctor; your father has gone black in the face!" (The reader is reminded about why Charlie was black in the face.)

Both of the older Stannard children, when later recalled to the witness stand, testified that their mother had, some two or three years before, ordered some anti-drinking powders obtained from the Montgomery Ward Catalog for the purpose of administering it to her husband in his coffee or tea. Both children testified that the maid knew of this "powder,": but when recalled later, Dolly Hammes denied any knowledge of anti-drinking powders. Clearly someone was not telling the truth.

Late in the trial, Judge Flannigan changed his ruling and allowed the words spoken by the victim, Charlie Stannard, to be introduced into evidence. Over **loud objections** by O'Brien for the defense, this ruling was sustained. Now, for the first time, the last words of Charles Stannard could be placed before the jury which was judging Laura Stannard on the charge of murder!

The maid, Dolly Hammes, was recalled again and questioned further. She told of Stannard's spoken belief that there was something wrong with his coffee that morning and that he felt he had been poisoned. With the conclusion of this last bit of testimony, the Prosecution rested its case against the accused.

Laura Stannard, after nearly three weeks of trial followed by her nearly five months in jail, appeared wasted and almost numb to her surroundings. Gone was the smile to the reporters during recess. She wept almost constantly during the final proceedings. There was little attempt to keep up her appearances, and her haggard face brought forth feelings of pity for her from the courtroom observers.

Patrick O'Brien for the defense began to build a case of suicide on the part of the deceased. He created an image of Charles as a hard-drinking wife abuser who felt sorry for himself because of his own failures as a provider for his family. Numerous witnesses were summoned who testified to seeing Stannard drunk and abusive.

Statements attributed to Stannard made through the years were recalled. The statement, "I often feel like going out into the woods and taking poison or shooting myself with a gun. I love my wife, but I don't think she loves me." was given in testimony by a Mrs. Cox, a neighbor, in recalling Stannard's words on the witness stand.

Mrs. Alexander, a witness described by the Herald reporter as being an "attractive blond" testified that she had once met Stannard at a local saloon where she had gone to pay a bill. She told of having a glass of wine with Charlie while he discussed his home life. He confided to Mrs. Alexander that he wished he were dead.

Several witnesses told of Charles foul moods when he was drinking.

A Mrs. LaRochelle told of seeing Stannard take the tablets he used to "brace up" after overindulging. Stannard had stated, according to Mrs. LaRochelle, that

.... if I took one of them (the tablets) too many, I'd be a dead man."

Now, in a risky, yet dramatic gesture, the Defense placed Laura Stannard herself on the witness stand!

Laura Stannard told of her marriage to Charles Stannard; of his kindness to her and his fatherly concern and love for his children, when he wasn't drinking. She presented to the court the perfect picture of a bereaved wife and loving mother.

When cross-examined by the Prosecution, however, Laura Stannard showed a fierce defensiveness when certain allegations were raised about her reputation by prosecutor Van Slyck. It was suggested that Mrs. Stannard had carried on several affairs through the years with boarders in the Stannard home, and that she had engaged in a highly questionable relationship with a teacher in the Greenland High School! Laura Stannard raged back at Van Slyck until that line of questioning ended. She then regressed into her shell of isolation.

Though the Defense claimed that the evidence against Mrs. Stannard was largely circumstantial, the very case that was presented by the Defense was based largely on testimony not directly related to the accusations.

Certainly there was a great deal of speculative evidence upon which to convict Laura Stannard, but was there real proof that the strychnine which had killed her husband had been administered to him by her actions?

Judge A.C. Flannigan cautioned the jury that to find a verdict of guilty, they had to find that the charge of murder was proved beyond a reasonable doubt...of course the term "reasonable doubt" is hard for a jury of lay people, unacquainted with the fine points of the law, to comprehend. The jury was out for only one hour and ten minutes.

Perhaps, after one of the longest trials in the history of Ontonagon county, they were anxious to get on with their business, or perhaps they were swayed by the pitiful appearance of the accused. Perhaps they were simply unconvinced by the rather circumstantial evidence presented by the Prosecution.

Perhaps ..... Perhaps ..... Perhaps .....

Whatever the case may have been, the jury returned with a verdict of "not guilty."

Laura almost immediately snapped out of the stupor-like countenance that she had fallen into. Her transformation was sudden and dramatic, and she became at once animated and talkative. After court was adjourned, she approached the jury and warmly thanked the jurors for their verdict.

Several friends from Greenland were in the courtroom and she told them, "Thank God, this is what I have been praying for all the time." Indeed, perhaps it is what she had been praying for all the time. The ordeal of Laura Stannard was over, or was it?

The family left the community shortly after the conclusion of the trial and finishing up their personal business in Greenland. The house in which the Stannards had lived actually belonged to Charlie's brother, William Stannard, so there were only the personal furnishings to remove.

Laura Stannard left the area, taking her children with her. It has been said, in later years, both of the older Stannard children who had testified against their father's character...took their own lives. A sad postlude to this controversial tale of death.

CHAPTER FIVE
CIRCUMSTANTIAL GUILT

Wednesday, May 12, 1908, the C.M.& St. Paul work train was winding its way up the slight grade to the Diamond Lumber Company's camp when Lyle Ross, the conductor who was riding in the cupola of the caboose spotted what appeared to be a body lying in the woods about 50 feet from the tracks. The body was clearly visible, as there were no leaves on the trees in the early spring and there was still snow in spots on the ground.

The Sheriff and the coroner were notified as soon as the train returned to Ontonagon and that afternoon Sheriff Charles O'Rourke impaneled a coroner's jury and proceeded to the scene. There was indeed a body lying in the woods just off the tracks, and from all appearances, it had been there for some time. The corpse was face down, though the head was turned slightly to one side with the nose touching the ground. Near the body was found a clump of letters and papers, badly faded from the winter's snows, and in a pile of old logs that had been skidded up near the tracks was found a coat and vest. The vest had been cut up the back and was still buttoned.

The remains were removed to Ontonagon in a basket, given a hasty postmortem, then buried. The body was not identified at this time, but after lying out all winter and into the warm days of spring, one can well appreciate the Sheriff s haste in arranging burial for the poor deceased.

Inquiry at the Diamond Lumber Camp of one Elmer Boyd, the foreman, indicated that two men had left the camp in mid-winter following a row. One of the men had also either owned, or been in possession of a pistol which he would go out into the woods and shoot at bottles with. The names of the men were given to Sheriff O'Rourke who already suspected foul play.

Though the first brief examination of the body at the site had shown no signs of violence, later examination had detected bullet fragments in the scalp. A pinkish fluid had been reported to be dripping from a hole in the head. Sheriff O'Rourke now ordered the body exhumed for a second, and much more thorough examination, to be conducted by Dr. A.L. Swinton, whose unhappy lot it was to be taking his turn at being the Coroner and County Medical Examiner.

Dr. Swinton cut into the back of the skull and found two bullets, having entered from different locations, but lodged in the same region of the brain. The bullets. in fine condition, were found to be of .32 calibre size. Positive identification was made of the body at this time by a Mrs. Stella (Casper) Guzek who operated a boarding house in the Polish settlement (that part of Ontonagon Village between Paul Bunyan Avenue and Michigan St., bordered by 7th St. and the Airport Road).

Acting on the names given him by Elmer Boyd, the Sheriff had contacted Mrs. Guzek who knew most of the young men coming from Poland and many of whom passed through her boarding house. She identified the remains as being those of a former boarder, Joe Guzik. When asked about the similarity of the last names, she pointed out that her husband's name was spelled with an 'E' whereas the victim's name had been spelled with an 'I.' Mrs. Guzek recalled that the victim had stayed at her house with several others before Christmas and that on one particular occasion, Joe Guzik had gotten into a terrible argument with another young Pole named Albert Fogusinski. Guzik had apparently slapped Fogusinski in the face which set the other man off into a tirade of threats and curses. Fogusinski had cried loudly, so all in the house could hear; "What did you slap me in the face for? A man that does that does not live long ... I'll kill you; if I don't kill you today, I will buy a gun and shoot you!"

According to Mrs. Guzek, the boarder, Joe Guzik replied, "If I say one word, you will be in State Prison for life." He had then reportedly put his head down on the table at which he was sitting and said no more.

Apparently making up, Guzik and Fogusinski went out to the Diamond Camp and took jobs; Fogusinski working in a saw team. It was also known that Fogusinski, after working at Diamond Lumber for a short time, returned to Ontonagon and purchased from Andrew Halter of Halter & LeMoine Hardware a .32 calibre pistol and two boxes of ammunition for which he had paid $4.50 in cash! Later, many at the camp recalled that in the evening when the day's work was done, Fogusinski would take the gun and walk some distance out into the woods and practice shooting.

In the evenings, many of the men at the Diamond Lumber Camp would play cards for low stakes, and shortly after Christmas of 1908, Guzik and Fogusinski got into a real argument over a card game. Threats were again exchanged but both men cooled down and no one thought much of it when first Joe Guzik, and then Albert Fogusinski asked for their time a short time later and announced plans to leave together. On December 27, 1907, both men drew their final pay and set off on foot.

Sheriff O'Rourke had never found a paycheck on Guzik's body, so he checked with the bookkeeper at Diamond Lumber. Both men's checks had been cashed and the canceled checks had been returned. Fogusinski's was for $45.31; Guzik's for

$44.80. What was quite interesting, however, was that upon examination of the canceled checks, the endorsements of both checks were in the same handwriting. Both paychecks had been cashed in two different saloons in Ontonagon in late December.

Convinced that Fogusinski must be found, Sheriff O'Rourke did a bit of detective work. He learned that in the small town of Sobieski (near Green Bay) a sister of the suspect lived. O'Rourke himself went there and obtained from the children who were home (the sister herself not being at home at the time) the address of another sister in Detroit. The Ontonagon County Sheriff then went to Milwaukee, following a lead given him by a half-brother who lived in Green Bay. In Milwaukee, the Sheriff learned that Fogusinski, working under the name of John (rather than Albert) had been employed a short time in a tannery, leaving unpaid bills and board behind him.

O'Rourke now went on to Detroit and called upon the Detroit Police for aid. He was assigned to a former Hancock man named Henry Bodinis, now a Detroit detective who spoke Polish. Detective Bodinis and Sheriff O'Rourke now went together to the address that had been given the Sheriff by the children in Sobieski. Bodinis knocked on the door and found the suspect inside. He invited Fogusinski to "take a little walk," and when on the street, Sheriff O'Rourke placed him under arrest and handcuffed him.

Fogusinski made no resistance and was held in the Detroit Jail overnight. O'Rourke then brought his prisoner back to Ontonagon, going by way of the Straits so as not to have to go the way of Wisconsin and take a prisoner across three states with the inherent red tape that would involve.

When arrested, Fogusinski had in his possession a pocket watch that had belonged to Joe Guzik. The watch was identified by Harris LaVine, Ontonagon jeweler who had sold the watch to Guzik.

Now charged with murder, Fogusinski entered a plea of innocent, claiming that he had traded his pistol to Guzik for the watch. Furthermore, he claimed to have last seen Guzik in Ontonagon the day they had quit at Diamond, in the company of two other companions (who were just conveniently not available). Fogusinski claimed that they had parted company at McKinnon's Saloon on December 28th and he had not seen Joe Guzik since that time.

Further investigation on the part of Sheriff O'Rourke had uncovered quite a record for Fogusinski. He was, at age 28 wanted on a serious charge in Detroit from which he had fled before coming to Ontonagon. The Detroit authorities had only with great reluctance turned a man they themselves had an arrest warrant for over to a County Sheriff from the Upper Peninsula. Fogusinski had been in the United States for only four years after deserting from the Russian Army. It also became known that the man was living under an alias, and that his real name was Wojak Bagashinski.

Ontonagon Circuit Judge Samuel Cooper presided over the trial in which he referred to the accused as a "Polander and a deserter."

Albert Fogusinski, alias Wojak Bagashinski was found guilty of first degree murder and sentenced to life in prison. His final disposition is unknown. In the words of the good Judge Cooper, "There was sufficient evidence to warrant the conviction, all of which was circumstantial. He had a fair trial and the jury was convinced of his guilt.

Fogushinski was accused of killing Guzik by shooting him from behind, as shown in this simulated scene.

CHAPTER SIX

DEATH OF THE JEALOUS HUSBAND

Young Henry (Hank) Picotte, age 21, was employed by the Spies-Thompson Lumber Company *making cedar*. He had been married to a young lady from Marinette for two years and the couple had a beautiful seven-month-old daughter.

On Saturday evening, February 6, 1915, Hank didn't come home from work. His wife, alarmed by his tardiness asked friends to go out and look for him.. He was found at his work site in the woods, lying face down in the snow. In his hands he held his new automatic rifle, in the back of his head was a bullet hole with a bullet exit wound through the top of his scalp. He had been dead for some hours when found.

Ontonagon County Sheriff Driscoll, upon examining the gun which had been Picotte's, found that the empty shell *was still in the chamber!* Now, the new fan-gled automatics weren't in common use at this time, but the Sheriff was familiar enough with the workings of such guns to know that it was virtually impossible for a shell to be fired and then left in the chamber.

There were many suspects in the case. Mrs. Picotte was a most attractive woman, and she had several admirers. Hank Picotte had been quite jealous and perhaps a bit over-protective of his pretty wife and was quite possessive of his little family. He was, however, a loving father and a good, steady provider for his family.

There being no solid evidence against any of the various suspects, the coroner's jury ruled the death to be an accidental shooting. Foul play was still suspected in view of the fact that it is quite difficult for a man to shoot himself in the back of the head, then to fall upon the gun holding it with both hands, plus the fact that the spent shell from this automatic rifle was still in the chamber. The only way the spent shell could be in the chamber was if somebody picked it up and put it back in the gun after it was ejected, and a person who has just shot himself in the head isn't likely to do that. From all appearances, someone was trying to make Picotte's death appear as a suicide, but for the reasons stated above, this was very unlikely.

Hank Picotte, very mindful of his family, had purchased and paid premiums on a life insurance policy with Northwestern Mutual Life for the sizable amount (in those days) of $1,000.00 With an accidental death verdict, the young widow was entitled to the full limits of the policy. The Coroner's jury rendered just such a verdict, which had been a manner of closing the books on questionable deaths in Ontonagon County for years. Being a rather close-knit community, and sensitive to the needs of the individual, *local officials have a long tradition of doing the right thing.* Picotte was dead and nothing was going to bring him back, but if a verdict of accidental death would help the widow collect the insurance (a suicide verdict would have voided the coverage in this case) and help her support herself and her child, then that was the way it would be.

Several weeks went by, then on Saturday, May 29, 1915 one Ralph Thompson, in a most agitated state and being described as on the verge of a nervous breakdown and also under the influence of alcohol, sought out Dr. McHugh and began to tell a terrible tale of sleepless nights and remorse at having committed a murder! Dr. McHugh immediately summoned William Cane as a legal witness and the distraught Thompson spilled out a tale of how he had taken the life of Henry Picotte that day in February.

Thompson had been one of those initial suspects against whom there was absolutely no evidence, and he had even testified at the coroner's hearing. Now, almost beside himself with feelings of guilt, he asked to be locked up. Sheriff Driscoll, though faced with a signed confession, was still reluctant to charge the man. Thompson, however, insisted that he had acted alone, wanted no one else implicated, and waived preliminary examination when finally brought before Judge Cyrus Spellman. What's more, Thompson made a most unusual request of Judge Spellman. He wanted to be sentenced at once without putting the County through the expense of a trial! *Never before had the law enforcement officials of Ontonagon County had such an enthusiastic confessed murderer on their hands!* The man clearly wanted to be punished, and quickly!

Ralph Thompson was not some nut! He was well educated, spoke well, and was a timber cruiser and estimator. He was good looking, large of stature and was still single at age 32.

Thompson was placed in the Ontonagon County Jail for safekeeping until the fall term of Circuit Court came up. He went to trial before the Honorable Judge Samuel Cooper in October of 1915. When brought before the court, he refused a lawyer and again requested immediate sentencing. Judge Cooper, completely taken aback at such an outlandish proposal, immediately turned Picotte's confessed killer over to Drs. McHugh and A.L. Swinton, both respected Ontonagon County medics, with the request of the Court that Thompson be thoroughly examined by the two doctors to determine if Thompson was sane enough to stand trial. In Judge Cooper's many years on the bench, *he had never heard of anyone demanding to be sentenced without a trial before!*

The two doctors, after spending several hours with the prisoner, concluded that he was quite sane and was fully aware of what he was doing and saying .... in short, he was completely competent to stand trial. In view of this finding, Judge Cooper appointed Chester W. Brown of Mass City as Thompson's defense counsel and Brown in turn approached W.G. Van Slyck as a special defense assistant. Never before had two attorneys had such a reluctant defendant to protect!

After a brief recess, the trial continued. The defense attorneys entered a plea of self defense, and now a tale as old as society began to unfold.

Thompson, taking the stand, related how Henry Picotte, in a jealous rage, had warned him about paying undue attention to his pretty wife! Thompson hurried to explain that he was acquainted with the young Mrs.Picotte, found her a pleasant person, and also adored the child of the Picotte's. It seems that on the day before Hank Picotte was found dead, Thompson had made a trip into Ontonagon for supplies, and among his purchases was a tiny sweater for the infant, which he had dropped off at the Picotte's cabin on his way back to camp. Hank Picotte had not been home at the time, but the young mother had accepted the gift and seemed glad to have any company stop by.

The very next day, Thompson had entered the woods in the area where Picotte was making cedar, perhaps to get an estimate of the cedar pile Picotte had produced. According to Thompson's testimony, Picotte was in a foul mood. He accused Thompson of all manner of improprieties with his wife stating in no uncertain terms that he was able to buy clothing for his own child and warned Thompson to stay away from his family.

Thompson went on: he walked away from Picotte about 64 paces (A timber cruiser is so accustomed to pacing off acreage that it was just second nature for Thompson to be able to state that he had taken 64 steps) when Picotte fired a gun at him! Thompson stated that he turned and fired back (he never explained how he came to be armed) at Picotte who was ducking behind a log on which he had been working. Thompson stated that he saw no more of Picotte; heard nothing, and fearing that Hank might be lying in ambush for him, he left the scene.

Ralph Thompson, the confessed killer of Henry Picotte must have told a convincing story, because the jury couldn't come to a conclusion. After several hours of debate, the result was a hung jury and on October 10 a retrial was ordered and Ralph Thompson had to wait a few more months to discover his fate.

While awaiting his second trial, Thompson, who had earlier wanted to spare the County of Ontonagon the expense of a trial, was an all-expense paid guest of the

County with free room and board!

The case drew a lot of interest in the community. February is the most desolate month in the Ontonagon Country as winter still holds the area in its grip, and spring which brings on the great breakup that spells the end of activities in the woods for the season is still a distant entity. A good murder trial was free entertainment for a town that had just passed a traditional U.P. winter and on Wednesday, February 8, 1916, there was standing room only in the courtroom on the top floor of the Ontonagon County Courthouse at the corner of Trap and Houghton. The eloquent trial attorney, M.J. Doyle of Marquette had been appointed as a special prosecutor to assist County Prosecutor John Jones for this trial ... Jones was determined to get a conviction this time around. Doyle lived up to his reputation and brought his full talents to bear on Ralph Thompson.

The Prosecution suggested that Ralph Thompson, seeing more in the relationship he had established with the victim's wife and child than really existed, had stalked Henry Picotte, and, using the victim's own gun, had shot him from behind and then replaced the spent cartridge in the chamber. He had then put the gun in the victim's hands to simulate a suicide or accidental shooting. Had Picotte's gun not been an automatic, perhaps he would have gotten away with the crime. Thompson had made the mistake of replacing the spent cartridge in the chamber, not understanding that an automatic *must eject the shell that has just been fired.* While drunk, he had confessed to the killing, then feigned insanity to escape punishment.

Defense attorney Chester Brown used the same basic defense strategy that he had employed in the previous trial; one of self-defense. The judge was the Honorable William Fead who had not sat on the case previously. Judge Fead took a full 40 minutes to instruct the jury before sending them into chambers, but this time the message must have been clear, for Ralph Thompson was granted his initial wish. *He was found guilty of murder in the FIRST DEGREE.*

Ralph Thompson, slayer of the jealous husband, was sentenced to life at hard labor at Marquette Prison.

The body of Hank Picotte was found lying in the woods near his work place, still holding the new automatic .22 that Henry was very proud of.

CHAPTER SEVEN

MASS CITY'S MURDEROUS MEDIC AND HIS LAST PATIENT

We have discussed previously the colorful past of Mass City, a wide open mining camp at the turn of the century. Mass City had a gun-toting Marshall, five times more saloons than Churches, and was the company town of the largest copper producer in Ontonagon County during that twenty-five year period stretching from 1900 to that time immediately following the Great War (WW I).

Among the professional people in Mass City was Dr. William Hanna M.D. who was a respected physician and healer of the sick and injured. Dedicated, hard working, and a thoroughly competent medical practitioner for his day, Dr. Hanna is still fondly remembered by many as the perfect stereotype country doctor.

There was another medical man in Mass City during the same period. Known as "Doc" Scott, this individual had a small and rather dingy office located near the railroad station. "Doc" Scott moved around from lumber camp to lumber camp, treating mostly lumber jacks. He toted a worn leather bag full of instruments, none too clean, that he used on various patients and was known to also treat sick horses with remedies out of the same satchel. Many said that "Doc" Scott didn't much care whether his patient was a human or a horse, the fees were the same!

Scott had a rather bad reputation for being a heavy drinker as well. On the wall of his office was displayed a fly specked credential, testifying as to his medical qualifications, but the document was not in English and no one bothered to inquire too much about Scott. His treatments seemed to work for the most part, and his fees were low, so people minded their own business. Scott never mentioned to anyone how he had lost his arm, but the elderly one-armed doctor was a familiar sight in the lumber camps and saloons about Mass City.

On the evening of March 2, 1915, Mrs. Fred Manninen (not the real name) died quite suddenly at her home. Mrs. Manninen had been experiencing some health problems, and was also pregnant at the time. She had just packed the dinner pails for her husband and her brother who were about to go on the night shift at Mass Consolidated, when she took violently ill and died before Dr. William Hanna, the Company doctor who had been summoned by the frantic husband, could reach the family home.

Dr. Hanna, who had served as County Medical Examiner for some time, thought the circumstances of the death warranted investigation. He did a post-mortem on Mrs. Manninen and personally took the stomach of the deceased to Chicago on the train for laboratory analysis. In the meantime, Fred Manninen, husband of the deceased, was arrested on suspicion of murder and placed in the County Jail.

Upon his return to Ontonagon County, Dr. Hanna made public the finding of the laboratory in Chicago. Mrs. Manninen had surely died of acute strychnine poisoning!

The full scope of the matter began to unfold as the formal investigation was conducted. It seems that Fred Manninen had gone to "Doc" Scott's office-pharmacy and asked Scott to give him something that would bring about a miscarriage of his pregnant wife. Scott had prepared a potion to accomplish what was requested and received payment for his services. Scott had warned Manninen that his wife would be come ill; would probably vomit, and may even faint, but not to be too concerned.

Mrs. Manninen had taken the "medicine" given to her by her husband, fully aware of what she was doing and in full agreement, according to her husband's later testimony, of the expected outcome. Shortly after taking the potion, she was afflicted with convulsions and vomiting and did appear to go into a faint. Alarmed, Manninen had summoned Dr. Hanna, but when Hanna arrived the woman was already dead.

When the circumstances became known, Manninen was charged with murder, but at his trial he managed to convince Circuit Judge Samuel Cooper that he did not intend to kill his wife but that the couple had sought to bring on the premature birth of the child that she was carrying. Manninen further agreed to plead guilty to manslaughter as he had certainly not planned the murder of his spouse. Judge Cooper gave Manninen a suspended sentence, feeling that the man had suffered enough anguish. Furthermore, there were two surviving children at home who needed a parent present. Manninen was placed on a five year probation, prohibited from leaving the state without the Court's permission, forbidden from entering any saloons, and required to pay a probation fee of $1.00 per month for the five years ... no small amount in those days.

The Court now had to deal with "Doc" Scott, the man who had actually prepared the deadly potion. The old man was arrested, brought before the court, and charged with dispensing illegal medicines, which was a misdemeanor. He was fined and his license was ordered revoked. Ha! "Doc" Scott didn't have a license to revoke! There was no way that Scott could be held legally accountable for the

the death of Mrs. Manninen as he had not, with his own hand, administered the poison which had brought about her death. The potion, it turned out, was a slightly watered down commercial rat poison!

A postscript to this story emerged in 1986 when a communication was received and forwarded to the Ontonagon County Historical Society from a relative of "Doc" Scott which shed a bit of light on the life of the man who had drifted into the mining camp of Mass City in the early days. Dr. Henry Scott (his real name) was born in 1839 which would make him aged 77 when he mixed the lethal "mis-carriage medicine" for Mrs. Manninen.

At one time he had operated two large drug stores in Bay City and at Saginaw, Michigan. He had received his medical training in Germany and had excellent qualifications as an apothecary. In 1887 the 49-year-old Scott had married 16-year-old Alice Rodden. The couple had three children, but the young wife left her hard-drinking husband because of his abusive ways. The 1910 Ontonagon County Census lists Scott as divorced. Scott practiced medicine later at Seney, then moved into the roaring town of Mass City where he remained until his death in 1917. He lies buried at the Maple Grove Cemetery.

In 1986, Scott's youngest daughter (who had been born in 1894) was still alive at the age of 92, but was still so filled with bitterness about her father that she wouldn't speak of him, the years having only served to intensify her feelings of loathing at the mention of his name. How very sad that drink and the rough ways of the copper frontier proved to be so overwhelming to a gifted man such as Dr. Henry Scott and reduced him to what he later became: a less than perfect physician and a troubled individual.

CHAPTER EIGHT
THE BEAN CAN MURDER OF 1921

To begin this story, you have to know that August (Gus) Karhu, a young Finnish immigrant of age 25 had held a grudge against his contemporary, Emil Hill, for over a year. During this time, many young men had come over from Finland and were employed as hired hands on farms in the Green settlement. On weekends, the fellows would all head for Ontonagon for a little R & R.

Gus Karhu, it seems, was known for having a rather quick temper, but Emil Hill had an even quicker knife, for Gus had suffered bodily injury at the hands, or rather at the blade of Emil Hill in a street fight the year previous. Gus' hand had been so badly cut that it had required the services of a local doctor to stitch it up. Let me tell you, when one of those Finnish boys had to actually see a doctor, it was serious! It seems that Emil Hill had also inflicted several wounds on Gus' neck and hands. There had been very hard feelings between the two since the fight.

On the evening of October 30, 1921, Karhu and Hill met, quite by accident, in a lunchroom in Ontonagon, but since there were several mutual acquaintances around them, and at the urging of the whole gang, the two enemies shook hands and *buried the hatchet*, so to speak; but later, some of those who had been present would say that they felt that neither Karhu or Hill was sincere.

Shortly thereafter, Gus Karhu left for Green, catching a ride with someone who had an automobile and happened to be heading in that direction. Emil Hill and a friend, Joe Saaranen also left for Green later that evening, riding in Orville Laine's car. The night was dark, without a moon, but also because of a thick fog along the lakeshore, the travel was slow on the winding road that led to Green ... the route of old M-64. Hill and Saaranen parted company with Orville Laine at the Green Store which Laine operated. Before taking leave, Emil Hill asked Laine to sell him a can of pork and beans which he opened on the spot. Saaranen and Hill started for home, along a woods trail, Hill eating his beans cold out of the can and drinking some of the juice as they walked along, talking.

Suddenly, out of the thick fog a figure, barely discernible, stepped into the trail in front of the pair. Joe Saaranen heard a sound such as a "melon being dropped on a hard sidewalk." He could see nothing, but could hear heavy breathing. Saaranen called out to his friend, Emil, but received no reply. He moved away a few paces and called out, "You'd better cut that out, whoever you are... !" Still no reply. In terror, Saaranen fled the scene and made his way to the place where he boarded, the Kaarna farm.

Saaranen related what had taken place to Mr. Kaarna and begged for a lantern to go back and look for his friend, Emil. Old Kaarna instead suggested that he get ready for bed instead, pointing out that there was "bad blood" between Emil and many others because of Emil's habit of drawing a knife at the slightest provocation. Kaarna added that it was probably a fight that wasn't any of Saaranen's business anyway.

Just at that moment, there was a LOUD pounding on the door and in burst a bloody Gus Karhu. Mr. Kaarna exclaimed that Gus must be pretty badly cut up, owing to the amount of blood on his clothes.

"Not me!" Gus replied. "You should see the other guy!"

Gus asked for water to clean up before going home to the place where he stayed. As he washed his face and arms, Gus Karhu bragged about being the one who had followed Emil Hill and Joe Saaranen along the woods trail, listening to them talk. He explained that he wanted to be sure he got the right man, so he had followed the pair for some distance before stepping into the trail and hitting Hill on the head with an iron gas pipe, then after Saaranen had left the scene, he had continued to beat Hill about the head until he was completely down, "knocking his teeth down his throat."

Gus then pulled a pearl-handled straight edged razor from his pocket and remarked, "This is a pretty good razor ... I found it in Hill's pocket. I finished him with it."

Old Kaarna, shaken, took Gus' pants which had been handed to him and washed them out in a pail of cold water. Gus put them back on, wet, and then fished in his pockets finding a handful of coins which he threw on the table, "for washing my pants." A small bottle of moonshine was pulled from his coat pocket and passed to Saaranen and Kaarna to have a drink. They were warned to keep quiet about what they had seen and heard, *or else*, then Gus walked into the night.

Joe Saaranen went straight to the Ontonagon County Sheriff the next morning. Sheriff James Fyfe came immediately to the scene and described it as a pool of blood on the footpath, as though someone has "stuck a pig," or slaughtered an animal. A few half-chewed beans and some broken teeth were found on the ground as well as a partly eaten can of beans. No body was found at the scene.

Given the testimony of Joe Saaranen, Gus Karhu was arrested. Hill's pearl handled razor was found stashed behind the mirror on the dresser in Karhu's room on the nearby farm where he worked and boarded. When interrogated, he refused to admit any involvement in the disappearance of Emil Hill, who had not been seen since that night. Without a body, there was questionable evidence to charge Gus Karhu with murder and bring him to trial, though he was indeed being held in the County Jail on suspicion of murder. After several months, a reward was finally offered to anyone who could either find the body of, or the whereabouts of Emil Hill. There was some speculation that Hill, beaten and disgraced, had left the area and was working in some lumber camp far out in the "boonies." Gus simply waited in jail and remained silent about the matter. Time was on his side.

In April of 1922, over five months after the incident on the trail, two young boys were crossing a swollen spring creek in the Green area. One of the boys was bragging to the other about what he would do with the reward if he found Emil Hill when just at that moment, the boy's boot lace hook snagged something in the water. Looking back, the young man was shocked to see another boot come up out of the water. In the boot was a foot with a leg attached! The badly decomposed body of Emil Hill had been found at last!

The face was badly battered and the throat had been cut nearly from ear to ear. The head just barely held onto the neck by a few strands of flesh. Even worse, County Prosecutor John Jones insisted that the local Coroner obtain some of the beans, still in the mouth of the victim, for evidence! The records on the case are quite thorough, true to a pattern of excellent crime investigation by Sheriff Fyfe. Gus Karhu was charged with first degree murder and brought to trial.

The jury brought in a verdict of GUILTY, and Judge George O. Driscoll sentenced Karhu to life at hard labor, then in a moment of rare pity for Judge Driscoll, he recommended parole review in the distant future. Gus seemed to not be aware of his predicament. His English was limited, and his own testimony was difficult for the members of the jury to understand.

As a footnote to this affair, Gus petitioned for a new trial in 1949, but was denied. In 1951, he again asked for a new trial and again was turned down. Finally, in 1962, Gus Karhu was given his freedom through a parole, after serving forty years for the murder of Emil Hill. He returned to the Ontonagon area and worked as a handyman and farm hand at Laitala's Dairy until the infirmities of age, aggravated by his years of penal labor ended his freedom for the last time. After going through the ordeal of a leg amputation, Gus Karhu died in the Maresh

Convalescent Home at Ontonagon in 1969 at the age of 73.

In his last years, when asked if he had killed Emil Hill, Gus Karhu, who had never admitted the deed, replied bitterly, *"Veri jouskee villa!"* ("His blood runs yet!")

CHAPTER NINE
THE LUNCH PAIL MURDER

On Thursday, April 27, 1922, 13 year-old Francis Panian, whose family lived at the Indiana Mine location beside the Copper Range Railroad tracks, set out for school at about 6:30 AM. The girl usually followed a route along the Copper Range tracks as far as the settlement of Lake Mine where she boarded the horse-drawn school jitney (bus) for the ride into Greenland where she attended school. She was reportedly a good pupil, having missed only one day of school that year.

Francis never arrived at school that day, nor did she return home that night. Her parents were not overly concerned, for Francis sometimes would stay the night at a friend's house. There was no telephone service to the Panian home, so the parents had no way of knowing for sure. They began to be somewhat concerned, however, when their daughter did not return home after school on Friday, but they had no reason to suspect anything was really wrong.

On Saturday morning, April 29th, her cold body was discovered by two local sawyers on their way to work. Seeing tracks in the snow leading to the powder house of the abandoned North Lake Mine, they followed the footprints up along the railroad spur to the building, curious to see who was poking around the old mine. The two came upon a young girl, lying on her back in the middle of the powder house floor, dead.

Sheriff James Fyfe was summoned to the scene at once and on the way, he called on Dr. William Hanna of Mass City who was the County Coroner. Dr. Hanna recognized the girl almost at once as one of his patients. Upon initial examination, Francis bore no marks of abuse, though there was a faint bruise on her right temple. She appeared simply to have lain down and died. There were absolutely no signs of a struggle. Hanna had the body brought to his office where he did a preliminary autopsy, noting that the bruise on her temple was not from a blow that was sufficient to kill her.

Sheriff Fyfe went out to Indiana Mine to break the news to the parents and to question them. Though quite grief stricken, the parents did their best to answer the Sheriff's inquiries. Mrs. Panian stated that she had packed her daughter's lunch and after having a good breakfast, the girl had left for school at the usual time. Francis had been in a cheerful mood and was looking forward to a day at school with her many friends.

It was the mention of the lunch that got Fyfe to thinking. There had been no lunch pail at the scene where the body was discovered. Fyfe assembled several deputies and began to walk the route the girl had taken to school. Near the railroad spur to the powder house, the lunch pail was found. The cover was off, and there were crumbs strewn about. A cup cake and a partly eaten sandwich were found on the ground. A practical man, Sheriff Fyfe wondered why the girl, having just left the breakfast table, would have began eating her lunch on the way to school? Furthermore, there was a strange odor emanating from the lunch pail and the food fairly reeked of the same strange smell.

Dr. Hanna, the Coroner, seized upon this discovery and began to look for poison. He removed several organs and sent them, along with the lunch pail to the state crime laboratory at Lansing. It was while doing this more complete examination that Dr. Hanna also discovered that the young girl has been sexually assaulted. The report was quick to come back ... Strychnia poison, probably in liquid form on the lunch and in the girl's vitals! However, the apparent amount of food eaten in no way accounted for the massive amount of poison found in the girl's internal organs. Baffled, Sheriff Fyfe summoned the Michigan State Police.

Detectives George Karkeet and Ernest Ramsey were sent to Ontonagon to work on the baffling case. They projected the poison lead a bit further and began a search of the area in which the body had been discovered for a container which may have held the poison. After a thorough combing of the area along the tracks, a small brown glass bottle was turned up, bearing a label with a skull and crossbones and the name of an Ontonagon drugstore. *There was also a faded number on the label!*

Following this lead, the Detectives called on Ostrander's Drug Store in Ontonagon where Ostrander, the pharmacist not only told them that this bottle had indeed contained strychnine, but also informed the Detectives that the bottle of poison had been purchased by John Panian, the victim's father some months ago! It should be pointed out for the reader here that strychnine was a commonly used poison by farmers and woodsmen for rodents and coyotes and was readily available over the counter in those days.

It seemed to the investigators, that someone was certainly going out of their way to point the finger of suspicion at the girl's parents: first the poisoned lunch, then the poison bottle itself with a clear trail to the girl's father. Was it indeed possible that the girl's parents had poisoned their own daughter? If so, for what possible motive?

The detectives drove out to Indiana Mine and questioned the parents further.

Did they have any enemies? Was there anyone they could think of who would want to harm a member of the family?

YES! There was a man who had boarded with the family for a time .... he had worked in a nearby logging camp. The man had developed an uncommon attraction to the 13-year old girl and had made several advances on her. John Panian had warned the boarder to leave his daughter alone, and though quite angry about the reproach, the matter seemed to end there. However, a short time thereafter, Panian had been reported for possession of an illegal venison and it turned out that the informer was none other than his boarder! Panian retaliated by reporting his boarder to the authorities for violation of the liquor law ... the boarder had been operating an illegal still in the woods with another man (Remember, this was during Prohibition). The boarder, in a rage, had left the Panian home, vowing to get even some day! The boarder's name: Joe Stimac, a Croatian who had a history of moving about from lumber camp to lumber camp, spending and drinking freely when he got to town.

The Detectives called on the last known place of residence for Stimac; a boarding house in Greenland where he had gone after leaving the Panian's. There the policemen interrogated a man named Chopp, the very fellow who had been charged with Stimac for operating the still. Chopp told how the men had made a pact to get even with John Panian for turning them in and also mentioned that Stimac had shown him a small brown bottle before taking his leave of the boarding house some time ago to "go to a farm job," but Chopp didn't know where.

Returning to Indiana Mine to question the parents further revealed that Stimac had gone back to the Panian place sometime before the death of the girl to pick up some clothes he had left behind. He had been told that his clothes were hanging in the basement stairway ... to take them and leave. The detectives asked John Panian if he had a bottle of poison. Panian went to the basement stairs and came back empty handed. His bottle of poison was indeed missing! *It just happened that it was on a shelf in the basement stairway where John Panian had kept his coyote poison.*

An all points bulletin was issued throughout Northern Michigan and Northern Wisconsin in an attempt to locate Joe Stimac. He was located working at a lumber camp in the Iron Mountain area. When arrested, he insisted that he had never been to Greenland in his life, but when he was confronted with his friend Chopp at Ontonagon he immediately claimed to speak no English and lapsed into Croatian. The Detectives can perhaps be forgiven for what they did next. After a few days in jail, Stimac, a chain smoker, was out of cigarettes and clearly in a bad way with nicotine withdrawal. One of the detectives entered the cell and slowly lit up a cigarette in front of the prisoner, then drew deeply, blowing smoke in the prisoner's face. Stimac actually licked his lips and inhaled deeply. "Oh, excuse me; would you like a cigarette, Joe?" asked the policeman, slyly. "I Don't mind if I do." replied Stimac, in perfect English!

In the face of this major blunder, Stimac asked to speak to a Priest. A Father Razek from Houghton who spoke Croatian was asked to come down and talk to the prisoner. After a short time with the Priest, Stimac opened up and confessed all. He told of his attraction to the girl ... she was described as being large and well developed for her age. Stimac told of how he waylaid her on her way to school and threatened to kill her if she didn't accompany him to the powder house. There he assaulted her.

In the words of Judge George Driscoll, the Circuit Court Judge who presided at Stimac's trial, "After bringing her to the powder house he sexually used her twice ... on each such occasion he forced her to drink some of the poison. He had her so terrified that she was willing to do anything he asked her to do if he would not kill her. He told her that the poison was medicine to prevent pregnancy. After forcing her to drink the poison a second time, he poured the remainder on her lunch which she carried with her."

Now, Stimac confessed to taking the lunch pail back to the railroad grade, tearing the sandwiches to make it appear that they'd been partly eaten, then tossing the lunch pail by the tracks to throw suspicion on the girl's father.

The *Ontonagon Herald* described Stimac as appearing to be about 65 years of age... "he is repulsive looking, quite gray, and had the look of a degenerate." (Imagine a newspaper printing a statement like that today and not getting sued by the accused!)

Judge Driscoll, in his summation of the trial stated, "This man, in my opinion, is heartless and soulless and a dangerous wretch whose only proper place during his lifetime is within prison walls. I might characterize him as a cunning and dangerous Croatian."

Joe Stimac received a life sentence from the jury who brought in their verdict on December 16, 1922. He served this sentence until his death at the Jackson State Maximum Security Prison.

Little Francis Panian lies buried at the Maple Grove Cemetery in Greenland. A portrait of the beautiful young girl was affixed to her grave marker, but the harsh elements have cracked the upper half of the picture and it is no longer visible.

NOTE: For further reading, the story of the murder of Francis Panian also appeared in the January 1943 issue of *Dynamic Detective* magazine under the title, "Death Riddle of the Deserted Mine" by J. Victor Bates.

CHAPTER SIX

DEATH AND MOONSHINE AT WHITE PINE

Ontonagon County certainly knows no barrier of the sexes when it comes to acts of violence or murder, as was shown earlier Chapter Four and in the account you are about to read. Women don't take a second place, either as the victim or the perpetrator.

White Pine, in 1929, was something of a ghost town. The community had been built during the boom copper years of World War I, and under the capable direction of Mine Superintendent Tom Wilcox, many company homes, a general store, a hospital, and a very modern surface plant had been created over the diggings that had first been discovered by the venerable Captain Thomas Hooper back in 1879. Calumet and Hecla had operated the mine until 1919 when falling copper prices following the end of the War brought about the mine's closure with only a few people remaining in the community living in company houses.

Hope for the community of White Pine, however, began to rise with the purchase of the White Pine properties by Copper Range of Painesdale, Michigan in May of 1929. It was now felt by many that White Pine would live again.

George Bentley was one of those who felt there was a future in White Pine. He continued to live in the community, and when he married, he brought his bride to White Pine to live. Now, before the reader pictures Bentley and his wife as a pair of young honeymooners, let me explain that George Bentley was, in 1929, 49 years of age and his wife was 38: the couple had been married for five years.

Because there was no obvious livelihood for a couple living in White Pine at that time, Bentley did what so many did in Ontonagon County during these Prohibition years. In the isolation of a community which was largely deserted, Bentley operated a most profitable moonshine operation!

One can only speculate on just what caused the arguments between husband and wife early on the morning of Wednesday, July 10, 1929, but the neighbors several houses away later testified that they heard quite a ruckus over at the Bentley's. You see, there is an unwritten code in Ontonagon County to the effect that a neighbor just doesn't get involved in a domestic argument, so the sound of the yelling, the breaking dishes, and the shouted curses were largely ignored by the Bentley's neighbors.

Perhaps the argument stemmed from the fact that George Bentley had been tried in Circuit Court only the week before, for violation of the Volstead (liquor)

Act, and had had to pay a pretty hefty fine. Perhaps it was the fact that he was continuing in this risky business of distributing moonshine, knowing full well that the Sheriff's men were watching him which led to the argument with his wife.

In any case, early in the morning of July 10, after several hours of argument and domestic strife, a rifle shot was heard coming from the Bentley home. Even then the neighbors did not interfere. Only when a hysterical Mrs. Bentley ran to a nearby house for help did anyone summon the Law.

According to the story Mrs. Bentley told the investigating officers, the couple had a serious "falling out" on Tuesday evening and as the hours went by, the argument became more and more serious. Apparently, George Bentley was actually threatening his wife with bodily harm. He had finally produced a loaded hunting rifle which was left lying on the kitchen table. Mrs. Bentley went on to relate that George was at one end of the table; she at the other...when in a fit of anger, he had lunged at her across the table, an upraised quart beer bottle in his right hand.

The wife went for the rifle and got off a shot from the hip. That shot brought her husband down, with a bullet through his neck. The Ontonagon County Sheriff had arrived on the scene and, upon entering the Bentley house, found George Bentley on the floor where he had fallen over backward after receiving his mortal wound. He lay on his back, still clutching a broken bottle in his upraised right hand, a look of surprise on his face.

The Sheriff was suspicious about the facts. In particular, he was puzzled about how a woman who was being threatened by an angry man with a bottle, could have calmly picked up a rifle ... an action which most women were not too familiar with in those days ... and coolly got off a clean shot that instantly killed her husband. The Sheriff theorized that there was reason to believe that Bentley had not been the attacker, but was only trying to disarm his wife who may have had the gun trained on him before he lunged at her across the table.

Because there were no actual witnesses to the shooting of Mr. Bentley, the distraught wife was placed under arrest immediately and charged with first degree murder. She was held without bail in the Ontonagon County Jail until her trial took place in October. At the trial, Mrs. Bentley entered a plea of innocent of murder and claimed self defense. It was pointed out that Bentley had on his person $390 in cash, a very tidy sum in those days. It was further pointed out that because of his illicit business in liquor, Bentley usually carried large amounts of cash. Mrs. Bentley had not attempted to escape, nor had she touched the money in her husband's pocket.

The jury deliberated a full ten hours weighing the testimony of neighbors and

CHAPTER ELEVEN
MASS CITY MOONSHINE MURDER

The date: January 26, 1930...Michigan Statehood Day. A quiet Sunday evening in Mass City was broken with the sound of a rifle shot, and the slaying of young Ed Savari by one Jonas Store.

It was a typical Sunday evening in Mass City, with five young gentlemen drifting about town, playing a little pool at Kermu's Pool Hall, then wandering out on the street to see what was going on. Finally, the young men wandered over to Jonas Store's shack. One must remember that this was still the Prohibition era, and a person had to be careful where alcoholic refreshment was procured. Jonas Store, a bachelor farmer who had a place out in Wainola, was known to produce a powerful but safe brew. It was also common knowledge that Jonas dabbled a bit in the sale of his intoxicating beverages. Store, a man of age 52, operated a farm, but on weekends he brought moonshine to town, selling the liquor to supplement his farm income. His shack on the main street of Mass City was something of a retail outlet for his moonshine.

When the boys arrived at Jonas' place, he was a bit hesitant to sell beer to such young customers, but did so. After a round or two, the boys were feeling pretty good and decided they wanted something with a little more kick. Jonas' straight moonshine was legendary in its quality and potency, and the boys now demanded the stronger stuff.

According to Jonas' later testimony, he refused the young men the hard liquor, and asked them to leave his place. At this point, the boys turned on him and beat him thoroughly, knocking a tooth right out of his mouth. They then broke open the cabinet where Jonas kept the "good stuff" and set about refreshing themselves, after all that exertion in beating Jonas up!

Store, seeing that his single resistance was futile, left his shack and crossed the street to seek help at the pool hall. He was ignored by Kermu and his customers. In a last attempt to get help, Store asked if someone would at least summon an officer. One must consider that Store was probably pretty desperate at this point, because calling in the Law would certainly subject him to a stiff fine for violation of the liquor law.

Still ignored, Store headed back to his shack, though now hardly able to see. His eyes were both badly swollen from the beating he had received. He entered his shack and made his way to the back room. The shack was in a shambles! The boys had scuffled among themselves, and knocked over the stove. Soot was everywhere, as well as broken dishes and wrecked furniture. The young gentlemen were so preoccupied with their libations that they didn't even notice that Jonas had returned.

Jonas went into the back room and felt under the mattress on his cot for his rifle. Finding it, he worked the lever several times to eject the cartridges from the magazine (according to his later testimony). Entering the front room, he leveled the rifle at the boys and ordered them to leave.

It was young Ed Savari who went for Jonas' gun and struggled to take it away from him. Suddenly, *the empty gun went off!* Young Ed fell to the floor. His friends, now thrown into confusion, ran from the shack, only to be met in the middle of the street by big Wilbur Kermu, who was now coming to investigate the sound of the shot. One of the boys attacked Kermu, knocking him down.

The boys now returned to Store's shack. Jonas was standing in the door with rifle in hand. One of the boys hit Store, knocking him down, and took his gun. The boy then ordered one of the others to keep him down as he entered the shack. His comrade, Ed Savari, was lying on the floor bleeding profusely from an abdominal wound. The young man, now quite sober, ran to Alanen's Restaurant to seek help, but no one present had a car to take the victim to the hospital. The same boy now ran over to Frank Uotila's Soda Parlor, but it was closed. Finally, at the Hautimaki Garage, someone suggested that the doctor and the sheriff should be called. Deputy constable Waino Turin was summoned at once, but by the time medical help could be brought, Savari was beyond help.

In the meantime, the ruffian who was trying to hold onto Jonas Store literally had his hands full. More evenly matched now, Store was putting up a good fight. Store had managed to get one of his young captor's fingers in his mouth, and locked on the boy's finger with his remaining teeth!

There were many circumstances involved in the charges and the defense. There was the matter of Jonas' serving beer to minors, and his well-documented past violations of the liquor law. There was the relatively clean record on the part of the young men involved. None of the boys who had been involved was really a serious offender or troublemaker.

The jury took a good deal of time deciding this case. Certainly there could have been no premeditation, or was there? After 25 hours of confinement in the jury room of the Ontonagon County courthouse, the jury came out with their verdict. Store was found not innocent, but also not guilty of the charge of murder. One can only wonder, with the laws of today, if the verdict would have been the same.